Today & Tomorrow's Blended Family

By D.R.Green

Today & Tomorrow's Blended Family
www.todayandtomorrowsblendedfam.com

Illustrated by Senitra A. Thompson
smashaundrest@gmail.com

Edited by
BJ Gray – BG&G Enterprises
www.bgge.com
Melva Robertson - The Write Media Group, LLC
www.thewritemediagrp.com

Copyright © 2017 D.R. Green
All rights reserved.

No parts of this publication may be reproduced, stored in a retrieval system, or transmitted in any form or by any means, electronic, mechanical, photocopying, recording, or otherwise, without the prior written permission of the copyright owner.

This book is sold subject to the condition that it shall not, by way of trade or otherwise, be lent, resold, hired out, or otherwise circulated without the publisher's prior consent in any form of binding or cover other than that in which it is published and without a similar condition including this condition being imposed on the subsequent purchaser. Under no circumstances may any part of this book be photocopied for resale.

This is a work of fiction. Any similarity between the characters and situations within its pages and places or persons, living or dead, is unintentional and co-incidental.

Dedications

Thank You Lord,
I will never forget that moment in my closet. I was crying out to you and praying about my next moves. Your response baffled me. You said, "Write a book, and I will do the rest." Well, here I am. I trusted, had faith and you delivered *Today & Tomorrow's Blended Family*.

Hubs,
Thank you for supporting me, loving me, making me the luckiest woman ever, and being my best friend. I look forward to having you by my side throughout this journey. I LOVE YOU.

Mason & Morgan,
You welcomed and continuously love on me. You guys have made being a bonus parent worth living and have taught me many things. Thank you for being who you are. I pray that you soar into young adulthood with integrity and humbleness, and that you work hard in your passions.
I love you guys.

Momma,
Hard work, perseverance, strength, and humor are a few things that you've taught me. Thank you for your support and unconditional love.
I appreciate and LOVE you.

To My Squad,
Thank you for always cheering me on. I have never doubted your support and will always be grateful for your transparency, advice, prayers, and laughter.
I love my "bridesmaids" and "honorary bridesmaids".

To My Family,
Your creativeness, wit, work ethic, love, passion for the outdoors, and compassion were ingrained into me since childhood. Thank you for making me who I am today. I LOVE Y'ALL.

Rest in Paradise
Betty, Ophelia, Willie, Juanita, Jewell, Angie, Chelle & Charisma

Without looking back, Today climbed the stairs, trying to decide which room could possibly be hers. She turned, and there it was. She imagined the many perks of her room, especially the fact that it had two beds.

"I will get to have sleepovers, and my bestie, Morgan, can come over. We'll both get a bed! We can paint our nails, dance, and sing karaoke!" She thought to herself, "Oh my goodness this will be so much fun!"

Today was so excited she didn't notice her dad standing in the doorway.

When she finally noticed him, she ran to him yelling," Daddy this is the best room a girl could ask for!"

Her dad said, "I'm glad you like it. Sit down for a minute so that we can talk." The two sat together on one of the beds.

"You know Daddy and Mommy love you with all our hearts, right?"

"Of course, Daddy," Today answered with a big smile on her face.

"Well," he said. "You will be sharing this room with Coco, and all of us will be sharing this house. It's not just you and me anymore."

"I know you love Mrs. Tori, but I want you and Mommy to get back together. And I don't want to share my room with Coco," said Today as the big smile on her face faded.

With a puzzled look on his face, Today's dad said, "Honey, I never knew you felt that way. Where is this coming from? I thought you wanted us happy?"

"Yes, Daddy," she replied. "I want you guys happy together—all of us—me, you, and Mommy."

Today's dad hugged her and then said," Honey, Mommy and I will never be together again as a couple, but we have a great friendship to co-parent you. And that's what matters."

Today dropped her head as she listened.

"I have Mrs. Tori. We love each other," he explained. "And we both love you."

To avoid hurting her dad's feelings, she ran downstairs, grabbed her scooter, and rode down the street.

As tears rolled down her face, Today moved faster and faster down the sidewalk. As she was riding, she looked into the sky and noticed the biggest and brightest rainbow.

"Hey Missy, you need a helmet!" yelled one of her new neighbors.

She suddenly heard someone yell, "WATCHOUT!"

Immediately, she saw the rear lights of a car.

While she tried to avoid the car, she lost control of the scooter and crashed into a mailbox.

"Are you okay?" asked a voice.

Unaware of what happened Today said, "Yes, I think so."

She looked up and saw a boy about her age staring down at her.

"My name is Tomorrow," he said. "My bonus dad was leaving to pick up my sister from day care. You almost ran right into his car! Are you new to the neighborhood?"

"Yes, we are. Well, my dad and step mom moved here this week", she said with hesitation.

"Bye dad!" Tomorrow said, as he waved back.

Today gathered herself up and sat on the curb.

"I thought you said that was your stepdad?" she asked.

"We don't say that word at our house," he replied. "I say 'bonus dad' to strangers so that they know he's not my real dad, but he does the same things that my dad does. He loves me just like my dad."

"Does that hurt your real dad's feelings?" Today asked.

"No," he replied. "Well I don't think so. My dad and bonus dad get along well. When they first met, my real dad told me that Mr. Aaron may be my 'bonus dad' one day, and that I should respect him. I believe I'm lucky to have two dads."

"Yeah, but I'm not calling my dad's wife 'Mom'," Today replied with a frown. "I only have one Mom! I don't understand why parents must get divorced! They mess everything up!"

"My parents didn't mess up," replied Tomorrow. "This is the happiest I've ever seen them both; so, I like it. But it was weird, at first, living out of two homes with two different sets of rules. There were plenty of arguments over who would spend the holidays with me, and sometimes, I felt like I had to choose which parent I liked most."

"But how did your parents get happy? My parents don't speak to each other unless it's about me," asked Today.

"I don't know. It's like I woke up for school one day, and my mom was laughing on the phone with my dad," he replied. "So, do you play video games? You can come over whenever you want."

Not hearing Tomorrow's invite, Today started thinking about what would happen when she got home.

She stood up, grabbed her scooter, and made her way back home.

"See you later Tomorrow," she yelled.

The separation and divorce were not your fault.

When Today walked into the house, she saw Mrs. Tori unpacking boxes.

"Hi Today! Did you like your room? It took me forever to pick the perfect colors," said Mrs. Tori.

In a somber mood, Today replied, "I did, thank you. May I be excused?"

"Of course," she replied.

Today walked into her room, and Coco was there styling her doll's hair.

"Hi Today! Isn't our room awesome?" Coco asked.

With her head down Today began to cry, "Yeah, it's cool, but I wish I was at my mom's house."

"Don't cry, Today. It will be okay," said Coco.

"How would you know? You get to have my dad and your mom in the same house, all the time!" Today cried.

Coco hung her head.

Mrs. Tori and Today's dad, Marc, walked into the room.

They sat on the floor and gazed in Today's eyes.

"What's wrong honey?" Mr. Marc asked.

"I don't want this new family! I don't want mommy to be lonely! I don't want two houses! I hate divorce!" Today cried.

She buried her head in her hands. Marc began to wipe her tears and waited for her to get it all out.

He then said, "Today I understand that you are hurt, and I am sorry that this isn't going how you'd like it to go. It hurts me to know that you are unhappy. I love you and want the best for you."

Mrs. Tori added, "Today, I love you too, and there's nothing I wouldn't do for you, Coco, and Mason."

She looked at Mrs. Tori with a glimmer in her eye. "You love me?"

Of course, I do," replied Mrs. Tori. "Why wouldn't I?"

"Well, I just thought you liked me only because you are married my daddy," Today said.

"No honey, I will always love you guys and continue to show you how much, every day. We can't remove your pain; only time will heal your hurts. I have a bonus mom as well, so I know how you feel. I am so grateful that I have two moms. They are a treat to me," answered Mrs. Tori.

Soon after that Mason, Mrs. Tori's younger son, ran into the room.

"Did someone say treats?" He asked.

Everyone looked at Mason and laughed.

"Sure Mason! Would you kids like to help me make some cookies?" Mrs. Tori asked.

"Yes!" They yelled, and all three kids raced downstairs.

Mrs. Tori and Mr. Marc hugged and then followed them.

Bonus parents want love and acceptance too.

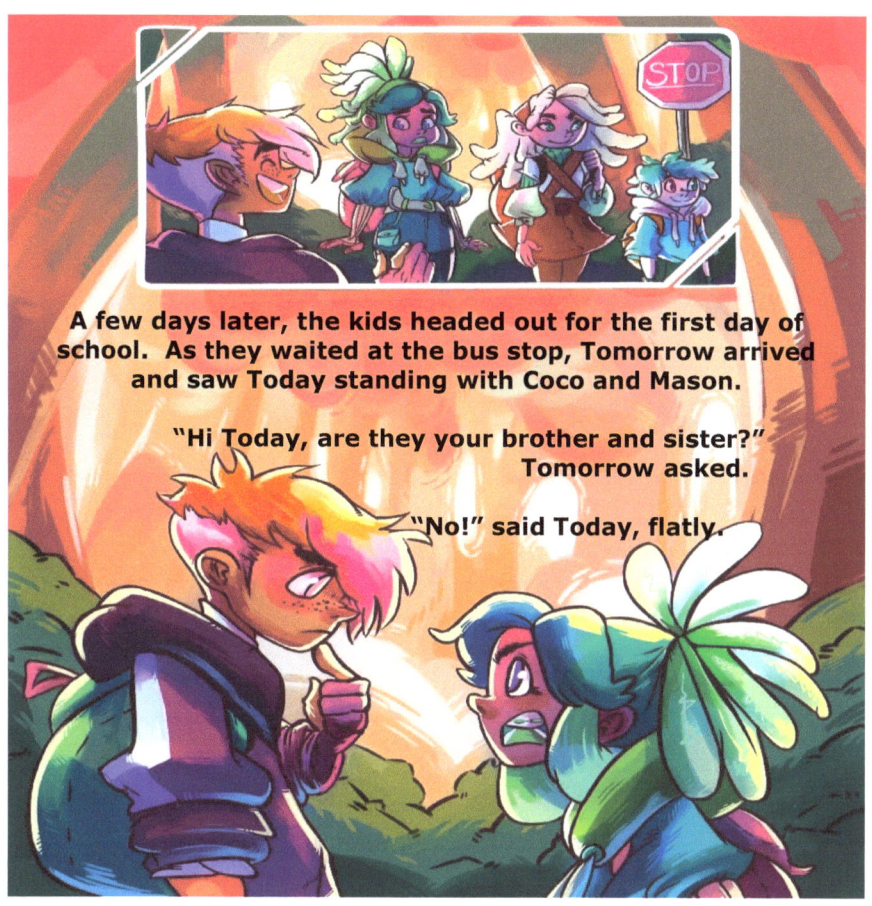

Tomorrow replied, "But I saw you guys coming out of the same house."

"Well, they are Mrs. Tori's kids," she answered.

Puzzled, Tomorrow asked, "Well, who is Mrs. Tori?"

"She's my dad's new wife," said Today.

"Okay. So they are your brother and sister," he said.

"No, they're not! We have different moms. Okay! Mr. 'I ask a lot of questions?' "

"Well, in our house my mom and bonus dad say if we're a blended family, we are family," Tomorrow replied.

Today said, "I see your point."

Coco and Mason look on with hurt in their eyes.

The bus arrived and, as the kids chose their seats, Tomorrow suggested that Today sit next to her sister Coco. Today agreed and sat next to Coco, but there was an awkward silence.

Coco said, "When my mommy went to the store, I asked her to buy our favorite snacks, so here's yours."

With sadness in her eyes, Today took the snacks and thanked Coco.

Today thought about how she had behaved towards Coco and asked, "Why did you do that for me?"

Looking down Coco said, "I've always wanted a sister. When Mommy told me we'd be sharing a room, it was like a dream come true. But I heard you talking to Tomorrow, so I get it. You don't feel the same way."

"Wellllllll I didn't really mean it," said Today.

Coco interrupted Today, "You're not the only person trying to adjust to our parents getting married. I've had tough times too."

"You do?!" Today asked.

"Yes! I remember watching you and Daddy Marc play the piano, and I wished that I could do that with my real daddy," said Coco.

"Where is your dad?" Today asked.

"My dad was in the military and died in a war when I was a baby. I have the pictures and stories from my family, but I don't have any memories like you have with your dad," she said.

"Wow, I didn't know that Coco. I'm really sorry," Today said sadly.

"It's okay. You're letting me share your dad, and he's super!"

Mason jumped from the seat behind the girls yelling, "Soup?! I don't want soup for dinner!"

The kids laugh as they arrive at school. Principal Pat and their teacher, Ms. Faye, greeted them.

Mason went to his class. When Today and Coco entered their classroom, they were greeted by a fun and squeaky voice coming from the corner.

"Hey girllllll….how was your summer?" asked Morgan, Today's best friend.

"It was cool. I moved and met this boy named Tomorrow. He's in the class down the hall. By the way, this is Coco. She's my bonus mom's daughter."

"Hi. Nice to meet you," Coco said with a lot of energy.

"Hmph!" Morgan said as she walked off.

"What was that about?" Coco asked Today.

Dreams come true in diverse ways.

Class began; Ms. Faye taught it. Afterwards, the girls went outside for lunch. Today asked Morgan if she could slide over, so that Coco could sit down at the table.

With a bite of her sandwich, she responded, "No!"

"What's wrong with you?" asked Today.

"Nothing. You obviously care more about Coco than your b-f-f. So no, there's not enough room over here," answered Morgan.

"I included Coco because she's my sister," explained Today. "If there's not enough room for her; then, there's not enough room for me!"

Morgan looked at Today with a puzzled look on her face. Today gathered her lunch and walked away.

Coco realized that Today was sitting at another table and hurriedly sat down next to her. She said, "Thanks for taking up for me Today But, ummm, why did you do that?"

"You're my sister, and no one treats my sister that way!" explained Today.

"I'm your sister?" Coco asked with tears in her eyes.

"Yes," Today responded. "If we are a blended family, then we are a family."

"That's very nice of you Today. Do I get to make an announcement that you're my sister in class? We're going to sit together in class and at lunch! Oh! I almost forgot about the bus," Coco said with excitement.

The girls giggled and headed back into the school. "Slow down 'mini me'. This is just the beginning," said Today.

The girls finished the day. As they headed for the bus to go home, Today bumped into Morgan.

"Sorry," said both girls.

"I apologize for treating your sister so badly earlier. I saw how happy you were with Coco, and I got jealous. I felt like she was taking my bestie away," Morgan explained.

"No, she can't take me from you. But she's my sister now, so you have to respect her in order for us to be friends. You should try getting to know her. She's pretty cool!" Today said with a smile.

"I can do that," Morgan said with an even bigger smile.

The girls hugged and went to their buses.

To make Coco's day even brighter, Today sat next to her on the bus. They both smiled harder than they had in a long time.

"Awww, look at the cool girl section, everyone!" yelled Tomorrow as he got on the bus.

As the first week of school ended, Today prepared to go to her mom's house.

Mr. Marc called upstairs, "Today your mom should be here shortly."

"Okay Dad!" Today yelled back.

Today was slowly putting some things into her bag. She looked at Coco, and Coco wasn't her usual fun and vibrant self.

"What's wrong Coco?" asked Today.

"I don't want you to go."

"Yeah, I thought I'd be bouncing off the walls and ready to go to my Mom's. But I'm kinda sad too," explained Today.

"That's okay." Said Coco. "Next week is going to fly by; then, we'll have plenty of time to catch up!"

"You're right," Today smiled.
The girls hugged. Marc yelled again, "Today your mom is here!"

Coco and Mason hung their heads out the window yelling their goodbyes.

Today's mom, Ms. Kia, waved back, and the kids watched until the car disappeared.

When they arrived at Ms. Kia's house, she was so eager to catch up with Today that she jumped right in with questions during dinner.

"How was your first week of school? Do you like your new teacher? Did you get settled in at your dad's new house? How are your new siblings?" asked her mom.

"Slow down mom. Everything and everyone is fine. But it started a little rough because it wasn't you and Dad. I believe we're going to be fine though," she explained.

"Well, sweetheart, it takes time. Not all mommies and daddies are meant to stay together forever. They move on with their lives and eventually find someone that makes them happier, like daddy and I have," explained Kia.

"Mommy, are you getting married too," Today asked.

"Now, you slow down. We can talk about that later. I want you to understand that Mommy and Daddy love you. We would only enrich our lives with someone else loves you as much as we do. I believe Mrs. Tori loves you that much! Do you believe it?" her mom asked.

"Yes, Mom. I believe it, and I love her too," said Today.

"Good! That's what matters. Now get ready for bed."

Today had a great week at her mom's, but couldn't wait to go back to her dad's house. Mason and Coco met her at the door like it had been a lifetime. As Today started getting settled in, the doorbell rang.

Mason called Today to the door.

"Hey, Tomorrow!" said Today.

"Hi, Today! We missed you at the afterschool program this week," he replied.

"I went to my mom's remember? I'm a car rider during her weeks," explained Today.

"Okay, cool. Grab your helmet; lets ride our scooters," he said.

Coco and Mason came running behind them. "We're coming too!" they both said.

Later that day, Mrs. Tori called the kids in for fresh lemonade.

The kids raced toward the mailbox, but something was odd about Today's screams as she got closer to the house.

Mrs. Tori could see that Today was losing control of her scooter. "Today, slow down!" Mrs. Tori yelled.

"I can't!" Today screamed with fear in her voice.

Suddenly, the scooter lost a wheel, and Today fell into Mrs. Tori's rosebushes. The kids ran to her rescue, but not before Mrs. Tori scooped Today into her arms and carried her into the house. Sitting in the bathroom, Today held her cheek and her knee.

"Okay. Okay. Let me see," Mrs. Tori said gently.

"Aww, look at that!" gasped Mrs. Tori as she dabbed the bruises with a warm towel. "You have a heart on your face!"

Today looked confused. "A heart?"

"Yes, although it's going to be a little sore for now. When it heals, it will look like a beautiful heart. And when someone asks you about it, you tell them that is the symbol of the love that so many have for you," said Mrs. Tori.

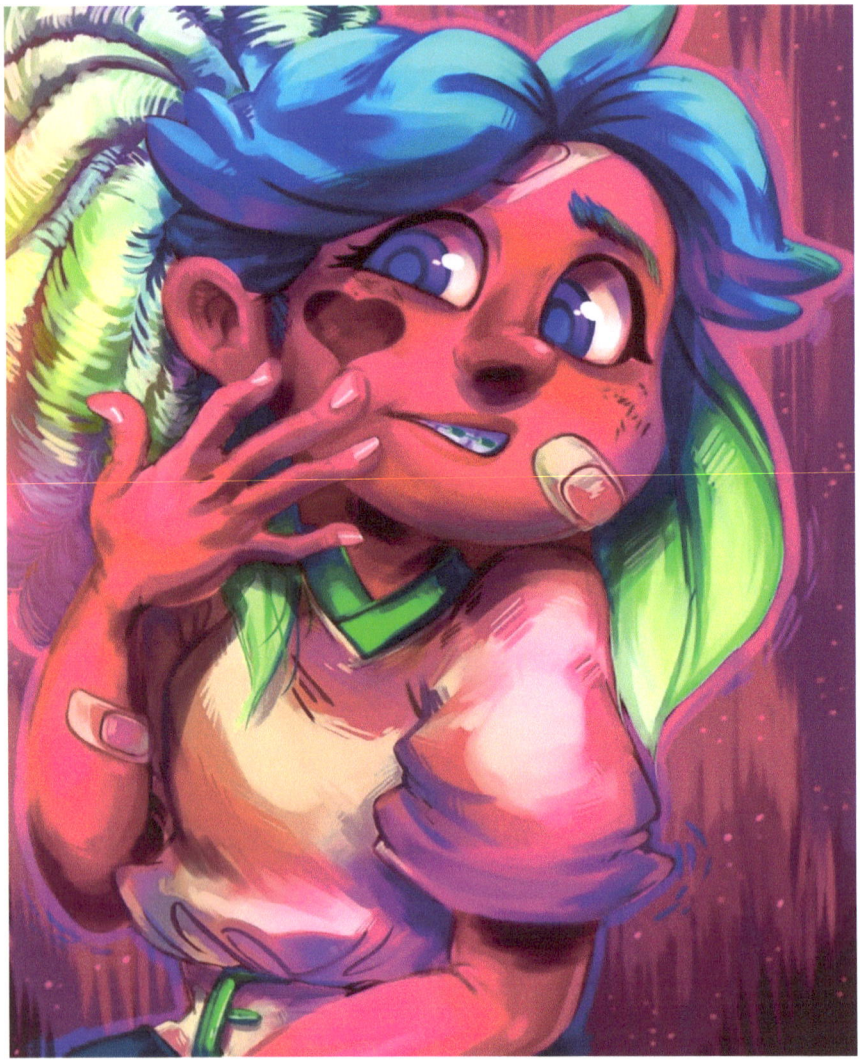

Today looked into the mirror and dried her tears.

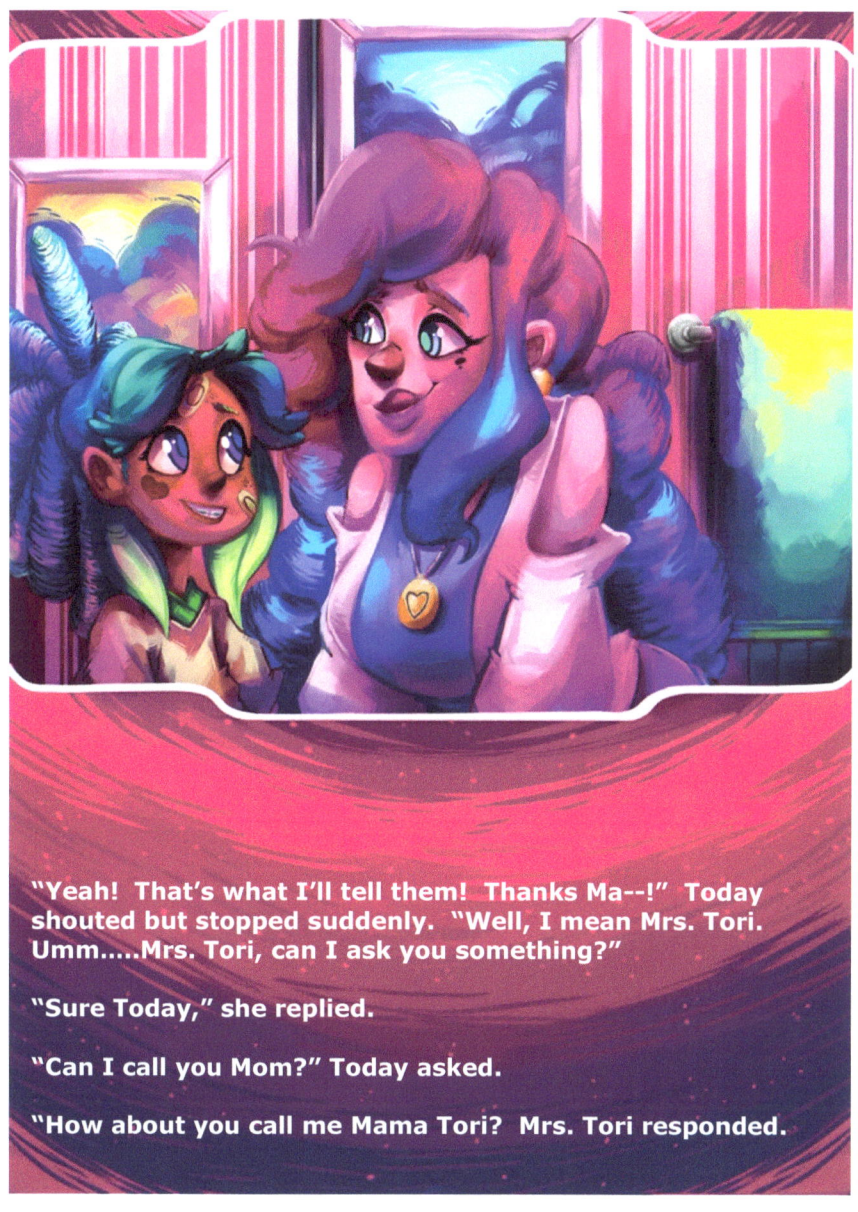

"Yeah! That's what I'll tell them! Thanks Ma--!" Today shouted but stopped suddenly. "Well, I mean Mrs. Tori. Umm.....Mrs. Tori, can I ask you something?"

"Sure Today," she replied.

"Can I call you Mom?" Today asked.

"How about you call me Mama Tori? Mrs. Tori responded.

Today smiled and hugged Mama Tori as hard as she could. Then she went back outside to play. Tomorrow was waiting on the porch.

"Are you okay, Today?" Tomorrow asked.

"Yes, I'm better. Mama Tori cleaned me up." she explained.

"You really scared her. I can tell she loves you," he said.

"You can?" asked Today.

"Yeah, she treats you just like Coco and Mason. We're both lucky to have that. I have other friends who don't, and they're always sad or angry," Tomorrow replied.

"Wow. I never looked at it that way," Today responded slowly.

"My dad taught me that it may rain today, but there's always sunshine tomorrow. Blended families aren't perfect, but we make it work because we're family," explained Tomorrow.

"That's right Tomorrow! Guess what? The sun is shining on Blendy Lane."

They smiled at each other and drank their lemonade.

The Beginning….

www.ingramcontent.com/pod-product-compliance
Lightning Source LLC
Chambersburg PA
CBHW041745040426
42444CB00001B/38